DOS - one step
at a time

BOOKS AVAILABLE

By both authors:

By Noel Kantaris:

DOS - one step
at a time

by

P.R.M. Oliver
and
N. Kantaris

BERNARD BABANI (publishing) LTD.
THE GRAMPIANS
SHEPHERDS BUSH ROAD
LONDON W6 7NF
ENGLAND

PLEASE NOTE

Although every care has been taken with the production of this book to ensure that any projects, designs, modifications and/or programs, etc., contained herewith, operate in a correct and safe manner and also that any components specified are normally available in Great Britain, the Publishers and Author(s) do not accept responsibility in any way for the failure (including fault in design) of any project, design, modification or program to work correctly or to cause damage to any equipment that it may be connected to or used in conjunction with, or in respect of any other damage or injury that may be so caused, nor do the Publishers accept responsibility in any way for the failure to obtain specified components.

Notice is also given that if equipment that is still under warranty is modified in any way or used or connected with home-built equipment then that warranty may be void.

© 1994 BERNARD BABANI (publishing) LTD

First Published – June 1994
Reprinted – March 1995
Reprinted – June 1996
Reprinted – May 1997

British Library Cataloguing in Publication Data:

A catalogue record for this book is available from the
British Library

ISBN 0 85934 327 8

Cover Design by Gregor Arthur
Cover illustration by Adam Willis
Printed and Bound in Great Britain by Cox & Wyman Ltd, Reading

ABOUT THIS BOOK

DOS - one step at a time has been written for those who panic about what to do next, when they are confronted with the DOS prompt on their PC computer screen. It is a very basic book and is not intended as a complete guide to DOS. No previous knowledge of computers, or of DOS operating systems is assumed. The book does not, however, describe how to set up your computer hardware, or how to install the DOS operating system. If you need to know more about the latter topic, or as a follow up to this material, then we suggest that you also refer to the books *A concise introduction to MS-DOS* (BP232), or *MS-DOS 6 explained* (BP341). For more advanced coverage, the books *A Concise Advanced User's Guide to MS-DOS* (BP264), or *Making MS-DOS Work for You* (BP319), may also prove useful. They are all published by BERNARD BABANI (publishing) Ltd.

This book can be used with any version of the DOS operating system, and is meant to simplify, supplement and, in some cases, to explain the documentation that came with your operating system.

The first chapter gives an overview of the history of DOS and lays the foundations for later chapters, which cover, one step at a time, the commands for handling discs, directories and files. A brief section on system configuration files follows, but without going into the complexities of memory management, and the last chapter deals with an introduction to simple batch files.

As with the other books in the series, this book was written with the busy person in mind. It is not necessary to learn all there is to know about a subject, when reading a few selected pages can usually do the same thing quite adequately!

With the help of this book, it is hoped that you will be able to come to terms with the DOS prompt and get the most out of your computer in terms of efficiency, productivity and enjoyment, and that you will be able to do it in the shortest, most effective and informative way.

If you would like to purchase a Companion Disc for any of the listed books by the same author(s), apart from the ones marked with an asterisk, containing the file/program listings which appear in them, then fill in the form at the back of the book and send it to Phil Oliver at the stipulated address.

ABOUT THE AUTHORS

Phil Oliver graduated in Mining Engineering at Camborne School of Mines in 1967 and since then has specialised in most aspects of surface mining technology, with a particular emphasis on computer related techniques. He has worked in Guyana, Canada, several Middle Eastern countries, South Africa and the United Kingdom, on such diverse projects as: the planning and management of bauxite, iron, gold and coal mines; rock excavation contracting in the UK; international mining equipment sales and technical back up and international mine consulting for a major mining house in South Africa. In 1988 he took up a lecturing position at Camborne School of Mines (part of Exeter University) in Surface Mining and Management.

Noel Kantaris graduated in Electrical Engineering at Bristol University and after spending three years in the Electronics Industry in London, took up a Tutorship in Physics at the University of Queensland. Research interests in Ionospheric Physics, led to the degrees of M.E. in Electronics and Ph.D. in Physics. On return to the UK, he took up a Post-Doctoral Research Fellowship in Radio Physics at the University of Leicester, and then in 1973 a lecturing position in Engineering at the Camborne School of Mines, Cornwall, (part of Exeter University), where since 1978 he has also assumed the responsibility for the Computing Department.

ACKNOWLEDGEMENTS

We would like to thank colleagues at the Camborne School of Mines for the helpful tips and suggestions which assisted us in the writing of this book.

TRADEMARKS

ACKNOWLEDGEMENTS

We would like to thank the ... at the Computers ... for the helpful hints and suggestions which assisted us in the writing of this book.

TRADEMARKS

DR-DOS is a registered trademark of Digital Research (now owned by Novell Inc.)

IBM and PC-DOS are registered trademarks of International Business Machines Corporation

Intel is a registered trademark of Intel Corporation

LaserJet is a registered trademark of Hewlett Packard Company

Lotus and 1-2-3 are registered trademarks of Lotus Development Corporation

Microsoft, MS-DOS and Microsoft Windows are registered trademarks of Microsoft Corporation

GXA Norton and Norton Editor are registered trademarks of Symantec Corporation

All other names and product names are trademarks registered trademarks of their respective owners.

CONTENTS

1. AN INTRODUCTION TO DOS

Every personal computer, whether it fits in your case, or sits on your desk, and of whatever make, is made up of two main parts:

HARDWARE   The physical system components, such as the screen, keyboard, disc drives, processors, etc.

SOFTWARE   Programs which are stored in files on discs. When a program file is 'run', a set of very detailed instructions is actioned, which take control of the hardware of the computer.

Word processors, spreadsheets, databases and games are all examples of programs. When such a program is running, it will control what actions are carried out when, for example, you enter characters from the keyboard.

Disc Operating System

DOS, short for 'DISC OPERATING SYSTEM', is a special type of software. It provides a range of commands to control both the system hardware and the storage of programs and files on disc. It does, in fact, form an interface between the hardware and software of a computer system. Other application programs use the facilities of DOS to control the PC on which they run. To a large extent this common interface has been the reason for the success of the IBM compatible PC.

Without an operating system you would not be able to access information stored on discs. When no other application program is running, you can use the DOS commands to manipulate files, discs and generally control your system, as will be described in this book.

Versions of DOS:

Three main software houses produce versions of DOS for use on IBM compatible PC computers. By far the largest is Microsoft, with MS-DOS. IBM market their operating system as PC-DOS and Digital Research, now owned by Novell, as DR-DOS.

Since its inception in 1981, MS-DOS has been the standard operating system for personal computers and by now is being used by more than 50 million people. As the number of users increased over the years, so too has the complexity of application programs run on their PCs. To meet these ever increasing demands, MS-DOS has also increased its functionality several times with *new* versions, as shown in the table below.

Version	Date	Main changes
1.0	1981	Microsoft renamed to MS-DOS the Original Disc Operating System 86-QDOS written by Seattle Computer Products. IBM calls this PC-DOS.
1.25	1982	Supported double-sided discs and fixed a number of bugs. IBM calls this PC-DOS 1.1
2.0	1983	Provided support for a 10MB hard disc, 360KB floppy discs and subdirectories
2.11	1983	Provided support for the extended character set.
3.0	1984	Provided support for 1.2MB floppy disc and larger capacity hard disc (up to 32MB).
3.1	1984	Provided support for networks.
3.2	1986	Provided support for 3½", 720KB floppy discs.

Version	Date	Main changes
3.3	1987	Provided support for PS/2 computer range, 1.44MB, 3½" floppy discs, partitioning of hard discs, and a number of additional codepages.
4.0	1988	Provided support for extended memory (EMS), hard disc partitions beyond 32MB (up to 2GB), and the graphical user interface DOS shell.
4.01	1989	Fixed bugs in version 4.0.
5.0	1991	Added the ability to run DOS in high memory and certain device drivers in upper memory. Included a full screen editor and context sensitive help, and supported the 2.88MB floppy disc.
6.0	1993	Included MSBACKUP, Double Space, Anti-Virus, and Defrag disc utilities. Added the Move & Deltree commands and provided for multiple start-up configurations.
6.2	1993	Improved safety with Double Space, which can now be uninstalled. Supports a one-pass DISKCOPY, and CD-ROM caching. The DOS shell was dropped from the package, and the CHKDSK command was replaced with SCANDISK.

At a basic level all these versions are compatible and the name DOS will be used throughout this book to apply to them all, including the IBM and Novell varieties.

The Structure of DOS

The DOS operating system consists of a collection of small, specialised programs that make up the working environment which allows you to create and save programs, copy or delete data files from disc or perform other input and output (I/O) operations, such as finding a program or a file on a particular disc.

To understand how to use DOS it helps to understand its underlying structure. The various DOS administrative functions are contained in three, separate, main files (later on, we will explain what files mean and their naming convention).

For MS-DOS these are:

```
MSDOS.SYS
IO.SYS
COMMAND.COM
```

The first file is the core of the operating system, while the second one, also called the Basic Input Output System (BIOS), allows the core to communicate with the hardware. It is the BIOS that is adapted by manufacturers of different PCs so that the operating system can appear to function in the same way, even though there might be differences in design.

The last file, COMMAND.COM, is the Command Processor which analyses what is typed at the keyboard, and if correct, finds and starts execution of the appropriate command.

Internal and External Commands:

DOS has 30-50 built-in commands (depending on the version), normally referred to as 'internal commands', instantly available to the user as they reside in memory. These, together with the rest of the operating system, occupy some of the system RAM (Random Access Memory), as they are loaded into memory on booting up, or starting, the system.

In addition to the internal commands, there are over sixty 'external' commands which are to be found on the System and Utility discs supplied by the manufacturer of the operating system. The machine program which makes up each of these external commands is saved in a *file* under an appropriate name with a .COM or .EXE extension to the filename (later we will discuss this more fully).

Amongst the many command files which make up DOS will be most of the ones listed below, the name, size (in bytes) and creation dates and times of which depend on the version of DOS you are running on your computer.

Filename	Extension	Size	Date	Time
APPEND	EXE	10774	30/09/93	6:20
CHKDSK	EXE	12241	30/09/93	6:20
COMMAND	COM	54619	30/09/93	6:20
DISKCOPY	COM	13335	30/09/93	6:20
FORMAT	COM	22916	30/09/93	6:20
KEYBOARD	SYS	34598	30/09/93	6:20
LABEL	EXE	9390	10/03/93	6:00
OS2	TXT	6358	10/03/93	6:00
PRINT	EXE	15656	30/09/93	6:20
QBASIC	HLP	130881	10/03/93	6:00
RESTORE	EXE	38342	30/09/93	6:20
SCANDISK	EXE	119761	30/09/93	6:20
SORT	EXE	6938	30/09/93	6:20
XCOPY	EXE	16930	30/09/93	6:20

Some of these files might have different extensions from the ones shown above, i.e. .EXE might appear as .COM in your system, as the extensions tend to differ for different versions of DOS.

Collectively, these internal and external commands make up the computer's Disc Operating System (DOS). Some of these commands will be examined in more detail in the following sections of this book.

Booting up the System:

Whenever you start your computer by switching on the power, the system is booted up, which is indicated by the appearance of a C> or A> prompt, unless you are running an interface.

On booting up a microcomputer, the following tasks are performed:

- A self test is run on its Random Access Memory.

- A check is made to see if a floppy disc is in drive A:, and if there is, whether it is a System disc (a disc that contains the two hidden MSDOS.SYS and IO.SYS files). If it is, it boots the system from the A: drive.

- If no floppy exists in drive A:, an attempt is made to boot the system from drive C:, if there is one, otherwise in the case of the IBM, it goes into Read Only Memory (ROM) based BASIC.

- Configures the system by executing the CONFIG.SYS file (more about this later).

- Reads the BIOS and the DOS operating system.

- Loads into RAM the COMMAND.COM file so that internal commands can be made available.

- Executes the commands within the AUTOEXEC.BAT file (more about this later), if one exists, otherwise it asks for the Date and Time which can be reset at this point. Pressing the <Enter> key, confirms what is displayed.

Should you receive an error message while these tasks are being performed, you must rectify the error and restart the process by pressing simultaneously the three keys marked **Ctrl**, **Alt** and **Del**, shown in this book as **<Ctrl+Alt+Del>**. This will perform a 'warm re-boot', in contrast to a 'cold re-boot' which is performed either when first switching the power on or pressing the 'Reset' button.

Discs

 While your PC is running it will also 'hold' the active program and data in its working memory, or RAM. However, as soon as you shut down the computer, everything contained in this memory is lost.

To store information more permanently, it must be placed on discs, which come in two main types:

FLOPPY DISCS Can be removed from the disc drive and come in several types and sizes.

HARD DISCS These are built into your computer and are usually inseparable from their drives.

These days most computers will have at least two disc drives. A hard disc, designated as drive C:, to hold the operating system, application programs and data files; and a floppy drive, designated as drive A:, to allow programs and data to be copied to, or from, the hard disc.

DOS can only be logged onto one drive at a time, but you can change this active, or current, drive by typing its identification letter, followed by a colon (:), at the prompt and pressing the <Enter> key. For example,

    C>**A:**

will change the logged drive, from C: to A:, and the DOS prompt will change to

    A>_

which indicates that the currently logged drive is now A:. All further commands which do not specify a different drive, will access drive A:. To revert back to the previous drive, simply enter C: at the A> prompt.

7

Files

 As mentioned previously, all information is stored on a computer's disc(s) in the form of files. If you buy a new application program, it will be made up of different files stored on floppy discs or, maybe, on a CD-ROM.

Naming Files:

In DOS, a filename consists of up to 8 alphanumeric characters (letters and numbers only) and can have an optional three letter extension separated from the main name by a period (.), but **no spaces**.

DOS does not distinguish between upper- or lower-case characters, so the following are all valid file names:

COMMAND.COM, **config.sys** or **Myfile**

Types of Files:

You will encounter two main types of files with very different properties. These are:

BINARY FILES   Hold their information in machine format, which can only be read by your application.

TEXT FILES   Contain only letters, numbers or symbols from the ASCII character set (also known as ASCII files).

The extensions .COM, .SYS and .EXE are the most common extensions of the files which make up DOS. These are all binary files and contain instructions which are executed directly by the computer. You should not try to modify their contents.

The extensions .BAT and .TXT usually indicate a text file. This type of file is produced by a text editor such as **Edit** or **Edlin**. You can easily view and edit the contents of such a file with these editors.

8

Directories

DOS helps you to organise your files on disc by providing a system of directories and subdirectories. Directories are like folders in a filing cabinet, where each cabinet drawer would represent a different disc. Placing similar files in their own directory makes them easier to find and access at a later date.

The key to the DOS system is the 'root' directory, indicated by the back-slash sign (\), which is the main directory under which a number of subdirectories can be created. In turn, each subdirectory can have its own subdirectories, as shown below:

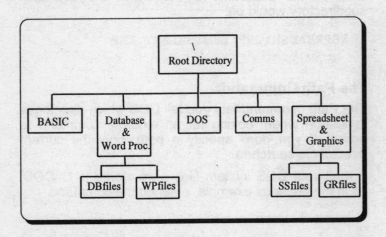

The root directory is shown with five subdirectories under it, while two of these have their own subdirectories. For maximum efficiency, the root directory should contain only the System and start up files, together with information on its subdirectories, a kind of an index drawer to the filing system.

Files in different subdirectories can have the same name because DOS can be told which is which via a system of PATH names.

DOS Paths

A path tells DOS how to locate a file within the directory structure.

A file in the SSFILES subdirectory of our example, could have the same name, say SALARY.TMP, as one in the GRFILES subdirectory. Nevertheless, we can instruct DOS to action the file in the SSFILES subdirectory by giving its path as part of the filename which is:

    \SPREADSH\SSFILES\SALARY.TMP

whereas the pathname of the file in the GRFILES subdirectory would be:

    \SPREADSH\GRFILES\SALARY.TMP

The Path Command:

The Path command lets you tell DOS which directories to search when looking for an external command to action. If you don't specify a path, only the current directory is searched.

If all your DOS system files were stored in C:\DOS, as in the previous example, entering the command

    PATH C:\DOS

would force DOS to search that directory every time it looked for an executable file until you either exited DOS, or set another Path.

It is usual to list all the directories to be searched in a Path statement in the AUTOEXEC.BAT system file, so that they are automatically available, as is explained in more detail later in Chapter 5.

Rules for Entering Commands

Commands can be entered in either uppercase or lower-case letters, but you must provide a space between the command and its parameters. For example, to obtain a listing of all the .EXE files on the floppy in the A: drive in wide format, you can either type

```
A>DIR *.EXE /W
```

or

```
A>dir *.exe /w
```

but you must type one space between the R (or r) and the asterisk (*). The asterisk here means 'all' filenames (it is one of the wildcard characters to be discussed later). The space between the E (or e) and the slash sign (/) is optional; its presence only serves to improve readability. The actual commands above will be covered in a later chapter.

If you make a mistake while typing a command, DOS will reply with the 'famous' message

```
Bad command or file name
```

when you press the <Enter> key.

You can easily edit what you previously typed by pressing the right arrow key (→) which causes DOS to display the last command one letter at a time. Keep pressing the right arrow key until you have reached the offending part of the command which you can then over-type. If need be, you can add extra letters to the command by pressing the <Ins> key, or remove surplus letters by pressing the <Del> key, then you can use the right arrow key again (or the **F3** function key) to reveal the rest of the command.

11

The DOS Prompt

Before we go deeper into DOS commands, make sure that your computer's prompt is of the form:

```
C:\>_
```

which indicates that the current directory is the root directory, shown by the back-slash (\). In this book, if we include the DOS prompt at the beginning of a command and ask you to type the command, make sure you DO NOT TYPE THE PROMPT; it should be already on the screen and typing it will produce an error.

Having a prompt which indicates the current directory is extremely useful because you can always tell whereabouts you are in your directory structure.

If your system is already configured, then an appropriate entry should exist within your AUTOEXEC.BAT file to produce this form of prompt. However, if this is not the case, then type

```
C:\>PROMPT $P$G
```

and press <Enter>. From now on, remember to press the <Enter> key whether you want to action a command you have typed. Without it, nothing will happen!

The PROMPT PG command should be in your AUTOEXEC.BAT file (to be discussed in Chapter 5), but before you can create or edit the AUTOEXEC.BAT file you will need to learn to use either **Edlin** (if you are a pre-DOS 5 user) or the **Edit** screen editor (available to users of MS-DOS version 5 & 6) or, indeed, any other editor or word processor, provided it can save files in text (ASCII) format.

2. WORKING WITH DISCS

When you purchase new floppy discs they are blank and usually unformatted. In this condition they cannot be used by DOS. Formatting checks a disc for areas (known as sectors) which might not be sound and, at the same time, structures the disc so that DOS can store and find data on it.

Formatting Floppy Discs

As long as you use the correct type of discs for your disc drive, a simple format can be carried out by using the following procedure:

1 Place the disc to be formatted in the A: drive.

2 Type the following command:

   FORMAT A:

3 Press the <Enter> key.

4 Then follow the instructions as they appear on the screen.

5 After the 'Format Complete' message appears on the screen, you are given the option to enter a Volume Label with a maximum of 11 characters. This is optional, if you don't want to label your disc electronically, just press <Enter> to skip the process.

With DOS 6 you will be updated continuously as the format takes place.

The example overleaf, shows the screen display produced when a 3½" HD (high density) disc was formatted in a high density A: drive of 1.44MB. Such a disc is formatted in 80 tracks with 18 sectors per track.

13

```
C:\>format A:
Insert new diskette for drive A:
and press ENTER when ready...

Checking existing disk format.
Formatting 1.44M
Format complete.

Volume label (11 characters, ENTER for none)? Data1

    1,457,664 bytes total disk space
    1,457,664 bytes available on disk

        512 bytes in each allocation unit.
    2,847 allocation units available on disk.

Volume Serial Number is 1840-1AE5

Format another (Y/N)?
```

Later versions of DOS give a formatted disc a Volume Serial Number, as shown above. You cannot change this hexadecimal number, which does not seem to have much use, except to DOS itself!

WARNING - as formatting a disc destroys the contents of that disc, you should use the command with care. Always double check what you are doing, before starting the procedure. This is especially important when you type the drive letter to be formatted. Losing the contents of a floppy disc may be bad enough, but if you type the letter of a hard disc instead, you are well on the way to a disaster.

As a safety factor most versions of DOS will display a message similar to the one below, if you attempt to format your hard disc.

```
WARNING: ALL DATA ON NON-REMOVABLE DISK
DRIVE C: WILL BE LOST!
Proceed with format (Y/N)?_
```

Formatting a Different Disc Type:

To keep your data intact, it is important that you do not attempt to over-format your discs. In other words to format 720KB capacity discs with 1.44MB.

It is easy to correctly format such a disc in a 1.44MB drive by using the following command:

```
FORMAT A: /f:720
```

but by default, DOS will attempt to format the disc the same as the drive type.

The /f:720 part of the command is a 'switch', which tells DOS to place 720KB of space on the disc. Some of the other switches for the FORMAT command are:

Switch	Purpose
/f:360	360KB double sided, double density, 5¼" floppy disc.
/f:720	720KB double sided, double density, 3½" floppy disc.
/f:1200	1.2MB double sided, high density, 5¼" floppy disc.
/f:1440	1.44MB double sided, high density, 3½" floppy disc.
/f:2880	2.88MB double sided, 3½" floppy disc.
/v:label	Specifies the label for the disc.
/q	Carries out a quick format on a previously formatted disc (available in DOS 5 or higher versions)
/s	Places the DOS system files on the disc, which can then be used to start up DOS on your PC (to boot the system from that disc).

Listing a Disc's Directory

To find out what files and subdirectories are in a directory, or on a floppy disk, you use the DIR command. The following step-by-step procedure would show the contents of a disc in the A: drive:

1 Place the disc into the A: drive.

2 With a 5¼" drive, make sure the drive door is closed. With a 3½" drive, make sure that the disc has clicked in place when you push it into the drive slot.

3 Type the following command at the DOS prompt

   ```
   DIR A:
   ```

4 If the drive door is not closed or the disc has not clicked in place, or the drive is empty, an error message similar to the following will display (depending on your version of DOS):

   ```
   Not ready reading drive A
   Abort, Retry, Fail?
   ```

5 If necessary, rectify the error and type **R** for Retry, or **A** to Abort the procedure. The **F** for Fail is used to change to another drive (such as C:) without having to insert a disc in the A: drive.

The directory listing of the disc in drive A: will then display on the screen, as shown on the facing page.

When used without switches, the DIR command shows the disc's volume name and serial number, followed by a listing of subdirectories and files, one line at a time, showing the size of each file and the date and time it was last modified.

This is followed by the number of files listed (with directories counting as files!), their cumulative size and the free space remaining on the disc.

```
C:\>dir a:

 Volume in drive A is DATA1
 Volume Serial Number is 14F9-2A15
 Directory of A:\

123          <DIR>           11/03/94   16:50
BASIC        <DIR>           10/03/94    9:40
COMMS        <DIR>           10/03/94    9:41
DBASE        <DIR>           10/03/94    9:40
DOS          <DIR>           10/03/94    9:40
GRAPHICS     <DIR>           10/03/94    9:46
WP           <DIR>           11/03/94   16:50
AUTOEXEC BAT          542    28/02/94    8:26
COMMAND  COM       54,619    30/09/93    6:20
CONFIG   SYS          395    26/02/94   12:40
TREEINFO NCD          203    11/03/94   16:54
        11 file(s)        55,759 bytes
                         984,576 bytes free

C:\>
```

If you use the above DIR command for a large directory, or a drive containing many files, the listing will rapidly scroll off the screen and you will only be able to read the last few entries.

To remedy this, most versions of DOS have the following two switches, which are demonstrated on the following two pages.

Switch	Purpose
/p	displays the directory listing one page at a time.
/w	displays the directory listing in a wide format across the screen.

DOS Version 5 and higher, have an extensive list of available switches, which enable you to fine-tune the DIR listing obtained. An easy way to check out these options, is with the following 'Help' command:

DIR /?

Listing in Wide Format:

To enable you to display large listings on a single screen, use the wide format option. This shows five entries, of files or directories, on a single screen line.

With this format the listing only shows directory or file names and extensions. There is no room for any more information.

To carry out this operation:

1   Decide what disc or directory you want to list. For example, to list the root directory of the C: drive from 'anywhere' on your directory structure, type

    DIR C:\ /W

2   Or, if you want to list the current directory, you need only type

    DIR /W

3   Press <Enter> to action the command, and produce a listing similar to that below.

```
C:\>dir /w

 Volume in drive C is NOEL'S_TOSH
 Volume Serial Number is 1B69-9D5A
 Directory of C:\

[123R4W]        [AMIPRO]        [BATCH]         [DOS]           [LOTUSAPP]
[NORTON]        [PAINTSHP]      [QA4]           [TD]            [TEMP]
[UTILS]         [WINDOWS]       SYM00001.$$$    COMMAND.COM     CURRENT.STS
EP.INI          LOGFILE.TXT     NORTON.INI      PORTMGR.COM     SD.INI
SYATDRUR.SYS    SYATPREP.EXE    TOOLS.INI       TREEINFO.NCD    CONFIG.SYS
AUTOEXEC.BAT
        26 file(s)         503,940 bytes
                         9,926,656 bytes free

C:\>
```

Listing One Screen at a Time:

Alternatively, with long listings, you can use the '/p' switch with the DIR command, to 'page' the display one screen at a time.

1   As before, decide what disc or directory you want to list, in our case we use the root directory of the C: drive.

2   Type the following command from 'anywhere' on your directory structure.

    DIR C:\ /P

3   Press <Enter> to action the command, and produce the first screen of the listing.

4   When you are ready for more, follow the instruction to 'Press any key to continue...'.

5   Carry on like this until the last screen appears, which in our case looked like that below:

```
Volume in drive C is NOEL'S_TOSH
Volume Serial Number is 1B69-9D5A
Directory of C:\

123R4W      <DIR>           22/10/93   18:42
AMIPRO      <DIR>           19/10/91   13:21
BATCH       <DIR>           18/03/89   11:48
DOS         <DIR>           18/03/89   11:33
LOTUSAPP    <DIR>           22/10/93   18:42
NORTON      <DIR>           18/03/89   12:03
PAINTSHP    <DIR>           11/06/93   15:23
QA4         <DIR>           18/07/91   12:40
TD          <DIR>           03/06/92   12:54
TEMP        <DIR>           16/07/93   14:10
UTILS       <DIR>           18/03/89   12:12
WINDOWS     <DIR>           25/02/91   20:29
COMMAND  COM       54,619   30/09/93    6:20
CURRENT  STS        5,190   14/02/92   17:19
EP       INI           37   26/02/92   15:54
LOGFILE  TXT        2,682   01/11/92   11:29
NORTON   INI          530   09/03/92   16:58
Press any key to continue . . .
```

Copying a Disc

← Slider

The external DOS command DISKCOPY, allows you to make an exact copy of a floppy disc, on another disc **of the same size and type**. This is very useful for making backup copies of your original application program discs, for safe keeping.

The destination disc does not even have to be formatted, as DISKCOPY can carry this out at the same time. However, because of this, any data on the disc you are copying to is destroyed, so you should use the command carefully.

Use the following procedure to copy a disc:

1 As a precaution, write protect the original disc, by either pushing up the plastic slider of a 3½" disc (shown above), or by covering the rectangular notch on the right side of a 5¼" disc.

2 Label the destination disc, and make sure it is not write protected and is of the same size and type as your original, or source disc.

3 Place the original in the A: drive and type

```
DISKCOPY A: A:
```

and follow the instruction to *Press any key to continue . . .*

4 When requested, change the SOURCE disc for the TARGET disc in the drive and press a key.

Depending on the size of disc being copied, and the version of DOS being used, the operation may require several disc changes. If so, be very careful not to mix the discs up. When the operation is completed you will be asked whether you want to copy another disc. Press, either **Y**, or **N** to return to the prompt.

The screen dump below was obtained using DISKCOPY with MS-DOS Version 6.2, which holds the copy of the source disc in a temporary file on your hard disc, until the operation is complete. It is then deleted.

This makes the process much quicker and means that only one disc change per copy is required, unlike earlier versions of DOS which require up to three disc changes for a High Density disc.

```
C:\>diskcopy a: a:

Insert SOURCE diskette in drive A:

Press any key to continue . . .

Copying 80 tracks, 18 sectors per track, 2 side(s)

Reading from source diskette . . .

Insert TARGET diskette in drive A:

Press any key to continue . . .

Writing to target diskette . . .

Do you wish to write another duplicate of this disk (Y/N)? n

Volume Serial Number is 1AE6-2655

Copy another diskette (Y/N)? n
```

If you have two identical disc drives, usually called A: and B: you can simplify the process by placing the source disc in the A: drive, the target in the B: drive and issuing the command:

DISKCOPY A: B:

You cannot, however, use the DISKCOPY command to copy from, or to, a hard disc or between two different types of floppy disc drives.

Comparing Two Discs

To find out if the contents of two floppy discs are the same, use the DISKCOMP command which compares similar discs on a track for track basis. To compare two such discs in the same drive:

1 Place the FIRST disc in the A: drive and type:

   DISKCOMP A: A:

   then follow the instruction on the screen.

2 When requested, replace the FIRST disc with the SECOND disc and press a key to continue. With High Density discs the operation may require several such disc swapping operations.

The screen below shows a successful comparison.

```
C:\>diskcomp a: a:

Insert FIRST diskette in drive A:
Press any key to continue . . .

Comparing 80 tracks
18 sectors per track, 2 side(s)

Insert SECOND diskette in drive A:
Press any key to continue . . .

Insert FIRST diskette in drive A:
Press any key to continue . . .

Insert SECOND diskette in drive A:
Press any key to continue . . .

Compare OK
```

The command only works with floppy discs, and only gives reliable results with discs whose contents have been copied with the DISKCOPY command.

3. DIRECTORIES

As mentioned previously, directories in DOS give you a way of organising your files into working groups. The DIR commands, discussed in the last chapter, can be used to view directories and their contents. Another way of displaying a more graphical map of the subdirectories and files in a directory is with the use of the TREE command.

Viewing a Directory Structure

To view the whole directory structure of a particular disc, carry out the following procedure:

1   Select which drive you want to view and make sure it contains the correct disc.

2   For a disc in the A: drive, enter the command:

    TREE A:

3   For any other drive on your system, substitute its drive letter for the 'A' in the above command.

The drive structure will display as shown below:

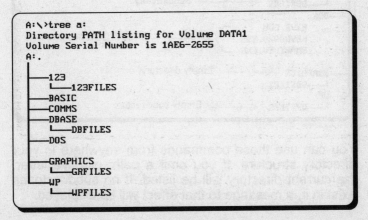

```
A:\>tree a:
Directory PATH listing for Volume DATA1
Volume Serial Number is 1AE6-2655
A:.
    ├──123
    │   └──123FILES
    ├──BASIC
    ├──COMMS
    ├──DBASE
    │   └──DBFILES
    ├──DOS
    │
    ├──GRAPHICS
    │   └──GRFILES
    └──WP
        └──WPFILES
```

23

Viewing the File Structure

To get a complete idea of the structure of a directory, or drive, you need to see what files it contains. This is easily done with the TREE command.

1 As before, select which drive you want to view and make sure it contains the correct disc.

2 For a disc in the A: drive, enter the command:

```
TREE A: /f
```

3 The switch '/f' produces a graphical listing, showing both the directories and files of the disc (in our case, the A: drive), as shown below.

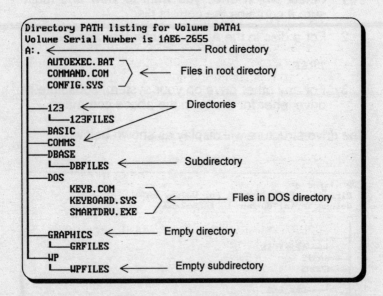

You can use these commands from anywhere in your directory structure. If you omit a path, or drive letter, the current directory will be listed. If no subdirectories exist in it, a message to that effect will be displayed.

Viewing One Screen at a Time

If you are using your computer with some of the suggested commands, you will have noticed that DOS commands which output information to your screen do not stop until all the data has been shown. Thus, long listings scroll off the screen far too fast to read.

The following procedure can be used to force the output to appear one screen at a time with any DOS command that outputs to your screen, such as DIR or TYPE (see next chapter). Below we use the TREE command to demonstrate it.

1   From anywhere in the directory structure, type the following command

    `TREE C:\ | MORE`

2   If the listing of the root directory of the C: drive is longer than one screen, it will stop when the screen is full with the line

    -- More --

    at the bottom of the screen

3   Press any key to scroll to the next screen, and continue doing so until the end of the listing.

4   If you are impatient to get on, you can terminate the process with the <Ctrl+Break> key combination. (Hold the Control key down and press the Break key).

MORE is a filter, and in our example, is separated from the main DOS command by the 'pipe' character '|', which is found at the bottom left corner of most keyboards.

As MORE uses a temporary file, it will not work if the disc is either full or write protected.

25

Filters and Pipes:

A filter is simply a command that changes the requested data, before it is output to the screen. The three main DOS filters are:

MORE   Displays the contents of a file, or a listing, one screenful at a time.

FIND   Searches for a specific text string in an ASCII, or text, file.

SORT   Alphabetically sorts the contents of a text file.

You use a 'pipe' in DOS when you want to use the output from one command as the input for another. You separate the two commands with the '|' symbol.

As an example of both these features the following command

```
DIR | SORT
```

would direct the output of the DIR command to the SORT filter, which would then send an alphabetically sorted listing of the current directory to the screen.

Redirecting Output:

Usually DOS sends the output from commands, or filters, to the screen. You can, however, redirect it and send it to a text file. This is useful if you want to keep a permanent record of the data.

To do this, you place a '>' symbol after the command, followed by the name of the file to hold the information, as discussed in the example on the next page. If the file exists, it will be overwritten with the new data. If it does not, it will be created by DOS.

Saving a Structure to Disc

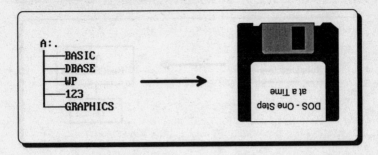

To save the directory structure to disc, do the following:

1 Select which drive you want to record and make sure it contains the correct disc.

2 For a disc in the A: drive, enter the command:

```
TREE A: /f > contents.txt
```

which will create the file *contents.txt* and place it in your current directory.

3 To place the file at another location you must enter a suitable path in front of the filename. For example, to place the file on the disc itself in the A: drive, you would enter:

```
TREE A: /f > A:\contents.txt
```

If you wanted to append the new data to an existing file, instead of overwriting the file's contents, you would use a double arrow (>>).

```
TREE A: /f >> A:\contents.txt
```

Using this technique you could very easily prepare a printed log of the contents of all your discs.

Creating a New Directory

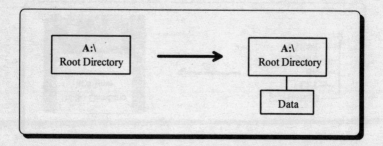

As an example we will build up a typical directory structure on a floppy disc placed in the A: drive. The procedure would obviously be the same for a hard disc, except the structure would be far more complicated.

1 Make sure your DOS prompt is set to show the current directory (by using PATH PG, as described in Chapter 1).

2 Place a newly formatted, or empty, disc into the A: drive.

3 If necessary, log on to the A: drive by typing

```
A:
```

and pressing the <Enter> key.

4 Your prompt should now show the root directory of A: as the current directory, as follows:

```
A:\>
```

5 To create a new directory, called *data*, enter the following command:

```
MD data
```

where MD stand for 'make directory'.

Changing the Active Directory

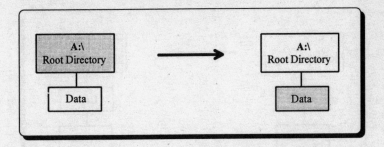

To make the new *data* directory the active, or current one, use the CHDIR (change directory) command, or CD for short.

Assuming that the prompt shows the root directory of A: as the current directory (if not see previous page):

1   Change directory by typing the command:

```
A:\>CD data
```

2   As soon as you pressed <Enter>, the current directory should change and the prompt should now display as

```
A:\DATA>
```

3   Create a subdirectory of *data* as follows:

```
MD wpfiles
```

4   Make *wpfiles* the current directory, as described above, which should display the

```
A:\DATA\WPFILES\>
```

prompt on the screen.

Moving between Directories

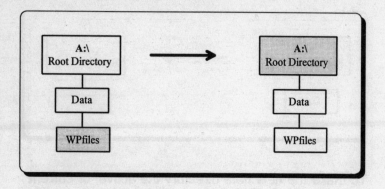

Making a subdirectory current (or moving down the directory structure to it) is simply a matter of typing its name after the MD command.

Moving back up the structure, however, cannot be carried out in the same way. You do not, in fact, have to remember the name of the 'parent' directory.

1 From the *wpfiles* directory, enter the command:

```
CD..
```

2 The prompt should change and indicate that the current directory has changed to *data*. Repeat the above command and return to the root directory.

3 If you had wanted to change straight to the root directory, the following command could have been used from anywhere on the drive:

```
CD \
```

4 If you know a directories path you can change to it from anywhere on the drive, for example:

```
CD \data\wpfiles
```

30

Deleting a Directory

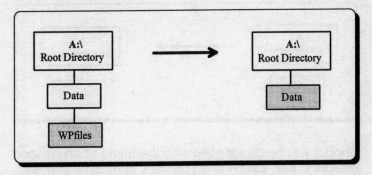

It is a simple matter to delete a directory from the end of the structure, as long as it does not contain any files.

1 Make *wpfiles* the current directory, as described previously.

2 Issue the following command to make sure there are no files in the directory:

   `DIR`

3 If the directory contains files, you cannot delete it without first deleting them (see next chapter).

4 Move to the parent directory *data* and enter the command:

   `RD wpfiles`

   where RD stands for 'remove directory'.

The DIR command should now demonstrate that the subdirectory has been successfully removed.

You should remember that you cannot use the directory navigation commands to move between drives. They only work on the active drive.

Moving a Directory

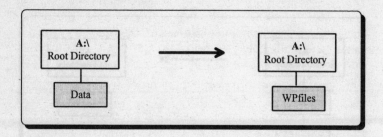

Should you be dissatisfied with the name of an existing directory, say, DATA and you want to rename it to, say, WPfiles, you can do so easily enough with the MOVE command, if you are a DOS 6 user. Pre-DOS 6 users cannot use this procedure, but see next chapter for an alternative method.

DOS 6 Users Only

1 Log onto the drive in which the directory you want to rename is to be found (in our case drive A:).

2 Return to the root directory from whichever subdirectory you are in at the time, by typing

    CD \

at the DOS prompt.

3 Use the MOVE command to move the \DATA directory, with all its contents to the \WPfiles directory (it *renames* the directory), by typing

    MOVE a:\data a:\wpfiles

If everything is successful, DOS responds with

    a:\data => a:\wpfiles [ok]

4. HANDLING FILES

The whole concept of DOS is based on files. The operating system itself, your data and all your application programs are stored in files. So the ability to be able to recognise, find and generally manipulate files is crucial.

If you spend most of your time working with a spreadsheet, database or word processor you will probably be quite happy using its file management facilities. There will always be times, however, when you need to use DOS to carry out certain functions. Hence this book.

Creating Files

There are many ways to create new files. Most of your application programs will create a new file the first time the SAVE operation (or its equivalent) is used. Such files would usually be binary and only accessible to their parent program. The DOS operations described here that deal with the contents of files are only applicable to text (ASCII - see Chapter 1) files.

Some of the ways of creating a text file are:

1 With the **Edit** full screen text editor, provided with MS-DOS Version 5 or higher.

2 Using **Edlin** with older versions of MS-DOS.

3 Using a proprietary text editor, such as the **Norton Editor**.

4 Saving a file in ASCII format (sometimes called DOS or TEXT format) from your word processor. This is possible with most such programs, as it provides a convenient way of sharing data between applications.

33

Copying a File

 You will probably often need to copy files around your system. There are several ways of doing this with DOS. The simplest is with the COPY command. You use this to copy files from one directory, or drive, to another. As long as you change the file name you can also make a copy of a file in the same directory.

The format of the COPY command is as follows:

```
COPY Source_file Destination_filename
```

For example to make a copy of the file CONFIG.SYS in the current directory and name it CONFIG.BAK you would issue the following command:

```
COPY config.sys config.bak
```

In fact this is a common operation which should be carried out before you make any alterations to any of the system control files.

To copy a file to, or from, a different drive or directory, you must include the full path of the other drive, or directory, in the command. Remember that the *source* path and filename is placed before the *destination* path and filename. The command

```
COPY monthly.rpt A:\
```

would make a copy of the file *monthly.rpt*, with the same name, in the root directory of the disk in the A: drive. On the other hand, the command

```
COPY A:\monthly.rpt
```

would copy the file *monthly.rpt* from the A: drive to the current directory and drive. In this case the destination (current directory and drive) are not even necessary.

Copying Files with Wildcard Characters:

When dealing with multiple filenames DOS lets you use two special characters as *wildcards*. These can both have multiple meanings and can be very helpful when you specify paths and filenames in a command.

The ? Wildcard

Using the query (**?**) character in a filename, means that any valid character can occupy that position in the filename. For example, assuming that there are several consecutively numbered files in your logged directory with filenames DOC1.TXT to DOC999.TXT, typing

```
COPY doc?.txt A:
```

will copy all files with the extension .TXT, from DOC1 to DOC9 to the disc in the A: drive. The files within the range DOC10 to DOC999 will not be copied. On the other hand, using two consecutive query characters in the filename, such as

```
COPY doc??.txt A:
```

will copy all files with the extension .TXT, from DOC1 to DOC99, but exclude those within the range DOC100 to DOC999.

*The * Wildcard*

Using the asterisk (*****) character in a filename, means that any number of valid characters can occupy that position in the filename.

For example, to copy all the files within the range DOC1.TXT to DOC999.TXT from your logged directory to the disc in the A: drive, type

```
COPY doc*.txt A:
```

Finally, the three character combination ***.*** which means 'all files with all extensions', can be very useful.

Copying Files from One Disc to Another

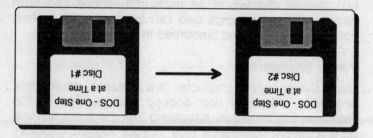

If you want to copy multiple files and directories, including lower level subdirectories (if they exist), from one disc to another, then use the XCOPY command. The general form of this command is as follows:

```
C:\>XCOPY source target [switches]
```

where **source** specifies the source file(s) or drive and directory you want to copy and **target** specifies the drive to which you want this source file(s) to be copied to. For example, typing

```
C:\>XCOPY A:\*.* B:
```

will copy all files in the root directory of the A: drive to the B: drive. If you only have one floppy drive, you will be prompted to change discs.

Some of the **switches** available are as follows:

/p	prompts the user with '(Y/N?)' before copying files
/s	copies directories and their subdirectories unless they are empty

XCOPY reads from the source disc as many files as possible into memory, before copying them to the target disc, unlike the COPY command which reads one file at a time. Therefore XCOPY is much faster.

36

Finding Files

Should you ever want to find out whether a particular file exists on a disc, just type its name after the DIR command. If the file exists, DOS will display its name, otherwise it will display the message

```
File not found
```

The full DOS command should also specify which drive and directory you want to access, but can be omitted if the command refers to the currently logged drive and directory.

Both the wildcard characters '?' and '*' can be used in the appropriate part of the filename, in case you are not sure of the exact name of the file you are trying to find. For example, typing

```
DIR doc*.*
```

will find all the files with all extensions on the logged drive and directory starting with the three characters DOC, irrespective of the ending of the filenames. The query (**?**) wildcard character can be used in exactly the same way as described in the previous section.

In general, the command

```
DIR doc*.*
```
or
```
DIR A:\doc*.*
```
will access all files starting with the letters DOC on the disc in the A: drive, while

```
C:\DATA\>DIR doc?.*
```
will access all files with a four letter filename beginning with DOC in the DATA directory of the C: drive.

Deleting Files

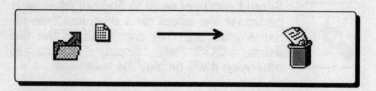

Sometimes it is necessary to make more room on your disc for new work by deleting unwanted files.

You can delete a single file by specifying its full name, or you can use wildcard characters to delete more than one file, from a list of files with similar name structures. However, to avoid deleting the wrong file(s), always follow the procedure given below.

1 Log onto the drive and directory where your unwanted files are held.

2 Verify that the file or files you intend to delete are indeed the ones you don't require by typing, say

```
DIR doc1.txt
or
DIR doc?.txt
```

3 If the listed file DOC1, or files (DOC1 to DOC9), are the ones you want to delete, type

```
DEL
```

and press the **F3** function key.

Typing DEL has the effect of replacing the DIR command and pressing the **F3** function key displays the rest of the previous entry following the DIR command. In this way there is no possibility of making a typing mistake and deleting the wrong files.

Renaming a Directory - Pre-DOS 6

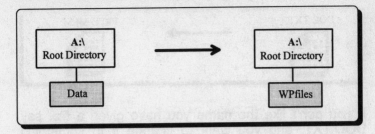

Should you be dissatisfied with the name of an existing directory, say, DATA and you want to rename it to, say, WPfiles, and you are a pre-DOS 6 user, then follow the procedure given below.

1 Create a new directory giving it your preferred name, say WPfiles, by typing

    MD \wpfiles

2 Copy to it all the files from the wrongly named directory, say DATA, by typing

    COPY \data*.* \wpfiles

3 Delete all the files from the unwanted directory by first using the DIR command, then typing DEL and pressing the **F3** function key, to display

    DEL \data*.*

4 Remove the unwanted directory from its parent directory by typing

    RD \data

This procedure is essential because prior to DOS 6, you could not rename directories from the system prompt, or remove directories unless they were empty.

39

Renaming Files

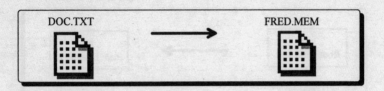

DOC.TXT ⟶ FRED.MEM

If you don't like the name you have given a file, say DOC.TXT, and you want to change it to something more meaningful, say FRED.MEM, then you can do so very easily by following the procedure below.

1 Log onto the drive and directory where the file you want to rename is to be found.

2 Type the rename command

   `REN doc.txt fred.mem`

The rename command is only used if the renamed file is to be placed in the same drive and directory as the original file.

If you want to rename a file and at the same time move it to another disc and/or directory, then either use the COPY command to copy it to the new location followed by the REN command if you are a pre-DOS 6 user, or the MOVE command if you are a DOS 6 user.

DOS 6 Users only

Assuming the file DOC.TXT is in the C:\DATA directory and you want to move it to the C:\WPfiles directory, type the following command:

   `MOVE C:\data\doc.txt C:\wpfiles`

DOS will respond with

   `C:\data\doc.txt C:\wpfiles\doc.txt [ok]`

40

Protecting a File from Deletion

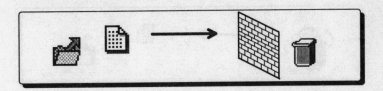

If you have a very important file which you would like to protect against deletion, then use the ATTRIB command below. This command sets the *read only* attribute of a file so that, although you can access and read the file, you cannot change it by writing to it.

Your system's configuration file CONFIG.SYS is a valuable file which you might consider protecting. To do so, follow the procedure below:

1 Log onto the directory where the file you want to protect is to be found. In the case of the CONFIG.SYS file this would normally be found in the root directory of the C: drive.

2 Type the following command

```
ATTRIB +r config.sys
```

Note that with this command, you type the attributes first, then you follow these by the drive/path and name of file you would like to affect.

For example, to set the *read only* attribute on a file DOC.TXT to be found on the A: drive in subdirectory WPfiles, while logged on the C: drive, you would type

```
ATTRIB +r A:\wpfiles\doc.txt
```

To remove the *read only* attribute from the above file, type

```
ATTRIB -r A:\wpfiles\doc.txt
```

41

Undeleting Files

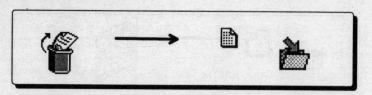

Users of DOS 5 and higher, can undelete a deleted file, provided action to do so is taken before any other files are saved to the disc.

Let us suppose that you have accidentally deleted a file called CONTENTS.TXT from your disc in the A: drive. Don't panic, do nothing else but type

```
UNDELETE A:\contents.txt
```

DOS responds with the following screen

```
UNDELETE - A delete protection facility
Copyright (C) 1987-1993 Central Point Software, Inc.
All rights reserved.

Directory: A:\
File Specifications: CONTENTS.TXT

    Delete Sentry control file not found.

    Deletion-tracking file not found.

    MS-DOS directory contains   1 deleted files.
    Of those,   1 files may be recovered.

Using the MS-DOS directory method.

    ?ONTENTS TXT      535 12/03/94 13:41  ...A  Undelete (Y/N)?y
    Please type the first character for ?ONTENTS.TXT: c

File successfully undeleted.
```

As you can see from the above, when you delete a file DOS deletes only the first letter of its name from its File Allocation Table (FAT), but not its contents. Provided you do not overwrite the file, you can undelete it by giving DOS the first character of the file's name.

Reading the Contents of a File

 If ever you wanted to read the contents of a text file, such as those in the two system files CONFIG.SYS and AUTOEXEC.BAT, then you could use the TYPE command. The command takes the following form:

```
C:\>TYPE config.sys
```
or
```
C:\>TYPE A:\contents.txt
```

if the file is not on the logged drive and directory.

The TYPE command is useful because it only lets you have a look at the contents of files without changing the environment in any way. Also it is much faster than using an editor.

If the text file you are looking at is longer than one screen full, then either use the <Pause> key, or the <Ctrl+S> key sequence (while holding down the <Ctrl> key press the <S> key once) to stop the scrolling of the display - pressing any key will start the screen scrolling again, or use the MORE pipe as follows:

```
TYPE autoexec.bat | more
```

You can use the TYPE command to send the contents of text files to the printer port with the command

```
TYPE autoexec.bat > PRN
```

where PRN stands for the 'printer' which is connected to the parallel printer port.

Using TYPE on other than text (ASCII) files, such as .COM or .EXE files, could cause your system to 'hang' after attempting to display sequences of machine code contained in the file. If that happens, use the <Ctrl+Alt+Del> key sequence to reboot the system.

Backing-up & Restoring Hard Discs

The pre-DOS 6 BACKUP command and the DOS 6 MSBACKUP utility allow you to archive important files from your hard disc and generate back-up copies on floppy discs.

The BACKUP Command - Pre-DOS 6 Users:

The external BACKUP command takes the form:

```
BACKUP source destination switches
```

where **source** is the drive/path/files to be backed up,
    destination is the drive to back-up to.
    switches are many, but the most useful one is:
    /s which allows the back-up of all the sub-directories of the source path.

Thus, to back-up all the word processor files whose path is \DATA\WPfiles, type

```
C:\>BACKUP C:\data\wpfiles\*.* A: /S
```

which backs-up all the files with all their extensions in the WPfiles directory and all its subdirectories.

The external RESTORE command is the only utility which can restore to the hard disc files previously copied to floppy discs using the BACKUP command. The RESTORE command takes the form:

```
RESTORE source destination switches
```

where **source** is the drive to restore from,
    destination is the drive/path/files to restore, and
    switches are many, but the most useful are:
    /p to prompt Y/N? before restoring, and
    /s to also restore files from subdirectories.

Thus, typing

```
C:\>RESTORE A: C:\data\wpfiles\*.* /P
```

restores selected files from discs in A: to the subdirectory WPfiles in the C: drive, *provided* these were backed up from the same named subdirectories.

The MSBACKUP Utility - DOS 6 Users:

The MSBACKUP utility comes in two versions, one for DOS and one for Windows. A graphical front-end controls all the functions once the program is started.

By default backed up files are compressed at a ratio which depends on the type of files being handled. In our experience word processor files with embedded graphics can compress at up to an 8:1 ratio, while binary files can compress to around 1.4:1. We have managed to backup a 17MB subdirectory onto only two 1.44MB floppy discs and in only a few minutes as well!

Configuring your System

Before using MSBACKUP carry out the following two steps. At the DOS prompt type

```
md C:\BACKUP
```

then enter the line below into the AUTOEXEC.BAT file

```
set msdosdata=C:\BACKUP
```

This sets a DOS environmental variable which will tell the MSBACKUP program where to find its configuration files, each time it starts up. Restart your computer to make the instruction immediately effective.

The first time you run MSBACKUP you get an 'Alert' message saying that Backup needs configuration. Press <Enter> to start the process, which only takes about five minutes. Accept all the video and mouse defaults, unless of course your system is non standard, in which case you will certainly know about it by now.

Your floppy and hard disc drives are tested and configured next, as is your main processor. You are then faced with the Configure dialogue box, from within which you should run the **Compatibility Test**, which carries out a small trial Backup and Compare operation to test the system. You will need two similar and numbered floppy discs.

To start an actual backup and restore procedure type

```
C:\>MSBACKUP
```

at the DOS prompt and select **Backup** from the opening dialogue box. This opens a further dialogue box from which you set all the backup options, select files to backup (by clicking them with the right mouse button - it might be necessary to **Exclude** all files and subdirectories, before using **Include** to make your selection), and choose the destination for the backup, which should be your A: floppy drive. Finally, check the estimated number of disks and space required and make sure you have that number of labelled disks ready, then click the **Start Backup** button to begin making the backup. If this button is greyed out, it means that no files have been selected for back up.

As part of the backup process, MSBACKUP creates a backup catalogue that contains information about the files you backed up and places one copy on your hard disk, and another copy on the disk or network drive that contains your backup set. When you need to restore any of the files, you need to load the backup catalogue set. Each catalogue set is given a unique name that helps you identify a backup set.

To restore your files and directory structure start MSBACKUP, and select **Restore** from the opening dialogue box. If the restoring is being carried out on a hard disc from which the backup was taken, then a catalogue will exist on the hard drive and will be loaded automatically.

If the original backup was carried out on another computer, or you have more than one catalogue set and you don't remember which is which, then you will need to copy it from the last floppy disc of the backup set by pressing the **Catalog** button and using first the **Retrieve** option to retrieve the required catalogue, then the **Load** option. Finally, right-click the **[-C-]** item in the **Restore Files** list to change it to **[-C-] All Files**, and press the **Start Restore** button.

5. SYSTEM CONFIGURATION

The CONFIG.SYS File

This file allows you to configure your computer to your needs, as commands held in it are executed during booting up the system. The easiest way to amend this system file is with the use of **Edit**.

If you are setting up your system for the first time, and depending on what version of DOS you are using, you might need to change the CONFIG.SYS file that is created for you by the SETUP program, because it might not include all the commands you will require to run your system efficiently. If your system had already run under an earlier version of DOS, then the SETUP program might have added some extra commands to your CONFIG.SYS file.

If your system has been implemented by, say, your computer staff, do not edit this file or use **Edit** to look at its contents, unless you have to and you know precisely what you are doing, as the file contains entries that DOS uses to define specific operating attributes. In this case, to view the contents of the file, use the **type** command, as explained earlier.

Some possible contents of CONFIG.SYS in a pre-DOS 5 version, are shown below:

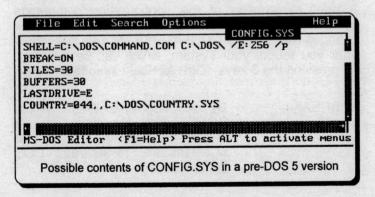

Possible contents of CONFIG.SYS in a pre-DOS 5 version

For a DOS 5 or DOS 6 implementation, the possible contents of CONFIG.SYS might be:

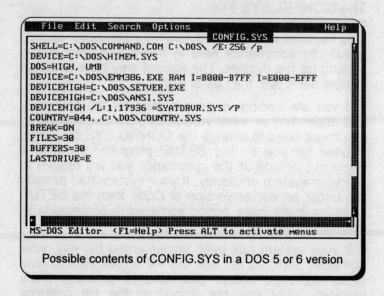

```
 File   Edit   Search   Options                              Help
                                  CONFIG.SYS
SHELL=C:\DOS\COMMAND.COM C:\DOS\ /E:256 /p
DEVICE=C:\DOS\HIMEM.SYS
DOS=HIGH, UMB
DEVICE=C:\DOS\EMM386.EXE RAM I=B000-B7FF I=E000-EFFF
DEVICEHIGH=C:\DOS\SETVER.EXE
DEVICEHIGH=C:\DOS\ANSI.SYS
DEVICEHIGH /L:1,17936 =SYATDRVR.SYS /P
COUNTRY=044,,C:\DOS\COUNTRY.SYS
BREAK=ON
FILES=30
BUFFERS=30
LASTDRIVE=E




MS-DOS Editor  <F1=Help> Press ALT to activate menus
```

Possible contents of CONFIG.SYS in a DOS 5 or 6 version

As seen above, under DOS 5 and 6, you can take advantage of high memory to load DOS and some device drivers into it, thus saving conventional memory.

Configuration Commands:

A brief explanation of the configuration commands used above, is given below. Do remember that any changes made to the CONFIG.SYS file only take effect after you reboot your system, which can be achieved by pressing the 3 keys <Ctrl+Alt+Del> simultaneously.

BREAK   By including BREAK=ON in the
                      CONFIG.SYS file, you can use
                      the key combination <Ctrl+C>, or
                      <Ctrl+Break>, to interrupt DOS
                      I/O functions.

48

BUFFERS

Allocates memory space in RAM to store whole sectors of data being read from disc, each of 512 bytes in size. If more data are required, DOS searches first the buffers before the disc, which speeds up operations. To change the number of buffers use

BUFFERS = n

where n can be a number from 1 to 99. Best results are obtained by choosing between 10-30 buffers.

COUNTRY

To change dates from the US format which is month/day/year to day/month/year, use

COUNTRY = 044

where 044 is for UK users.

Non UK users can substitute their international telephone country code for the 044. The default value is 001, for the USA.

DEVICE

DOS has its own standard device drivers to allow communication with your keyboard, screen and discs. Additional drivers can be specified to allow other devices to be connected. For example:

DEVICE = ANSI.SYS

loads alternative screen and keyboard drivers for ANSI support required by some software.

DEVICE = SETVER.EXE

sets the DOS version that DOS 5 and 6 report to a program.

49

DEVICEHIGH	Loads device drivers into the upper memory area.
DOS	Sets the area of RAM where DOS will be located, and specifies whether to use the upper memory area by including the command:
	DOS = HIGH
FILES	DOS normally allows 8 files to be opened at a time. However, some relational databases might require to refer to more files at a time. To change the default value, use
	FILES = n
	where n can be a number from 8 to the maximum required by your application which could be 30.
LASTDRIVE	Allows additional drives to be connected to a system, including the sharing of a hard disc on a network. The command is:
	LASTDRIVE = x
	where x is a letter from A to Z (default E).
REM	REM followed by any string, allows remarks to be entered in CONFIG.SYS. A semicolon (;) at the beginning of a line has the same effect.
SHELL	Allows for a 'front end' or an alternative Command Processor to COMMAND.COM to be used as real-mode command-line processor.

The command takes the form:

SHELL = FRONTEND.COM

where FRONTEND is the name of the alternative Command Processor. The default value of SHELL is COMMAND.COM.

The COMMAND.COM Processor:

This command starts a new command processor that contains all internal commands. This is loaded into memory in two parts: the resident part and the transient part which can be overwritten by some programs in which case the resident part can be used to reload the transient part. The command takes the form:

COMMAND [options]

with the following available options:

/E   specifies the environment size in bytes, with a default value of 160 bytes

/P   prohibits COMMAND.COM from exiting to a higher level

/C   executes a following command.

For example, the following statement

```
C:\>COMMAND /C CHKDSK A:
```

which might appear in a program starts a new command processor under the current program, runs the CHKDSK command on the disc in the A: drive, and returns to the first command processor.

DOS 6 users will have to use SCANDISK instead of the earlier CHKDSK.

The AUTOEXEC.BAT File

This is a special batch file that DOS looks for during the last stages of booting up and if it exists, the commands held in it are executed. One such command is the KEYB xx which configures keyboards for the appropriate national standard, with xx indicating the country. For the UK, the command becomes KEYB UK, and you will need to execute it if your keyboard is marked with the £ sign over the 3 key. The easiest way to amend this file, is with the use of **Edit**.

If you are setting up your system for the first time you might need to change the AUTOEXEC.BAT file that was created for you by the SETUP program, because it might not include all the commands you will require to run your system efficiently. If your system had already been running under an earlier version of DOS, then the SETUP program might have added some extra commands to your AUTOEXEC.BAT file.

Some of the possible contents of AUTOEXEC.BAT in a pre-DOS 5 version implementation are:

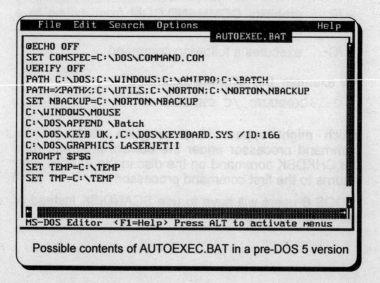

```
 File   Edit   Search   Options                    Help
                                    AUTOEXEC.BAT
@ECHO OFF
SET COMSPEC=C:\DOS\COMMAND.COM
VERIFY OFF
PATH C:\DOS;C:\WINDOWS;C:\AMIPRO;C:\BATCH
PATH=%PATH%;C:\UTILS;C:\NORTON;C:\NORTON\NBACKUP
SET NBACKUP=C:\NORTON\NBACKUP
C:\WINDOWS\MOUSE
C:\DOS\APPEND \Batch
C:\DOS\KEYB UK,,C:\DOS\KEYBOARD.SYS /ID:166
C:\DOS\GRAPHICS LASERJETII
PROMPT $P$G
SET TEMP=C:\TEMP
SET TMP=C:\TEMP



MS-DOS Editor   <F1=Help> Press ALT to activate menus
```

Possible contents of AUTOEXEC.BAT in a pre-DOS 5 version

Similarly, some of the possible contents of AUTOEXEC.BAT in a DOS 5 implementation, are shown below. In the case of DOS 6, REM out (or delete) the second line of the file, the one starting with SET COMSPEC=; you don't need it.

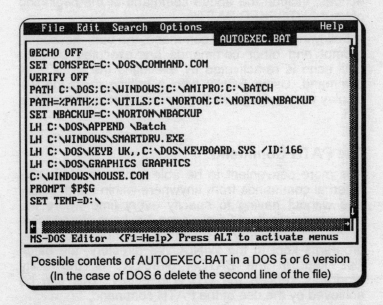

```
   File  Edit  Search  Options                    Help
                              AUTOEXEC.BAT
@ECHO OFF
SET COMSPEC=C:\DOS\COMMAND.COM
VERIFY OFF
PATH C:\DOS;C:\WINDOWS;C:\AMIPRO;C:\BATCH
PATH=%PATH%;C:\UTILS;C:\NORTON;C:\NORTON\NBACKUP
SET NBACKUP=C:\NORTON\NBACKUP
LH C:\DOS\APPEND \Batch
LH C:\WINDOWS\SMARTDRV.EXE
LH C:\DOS\KEYB UK,,C:\DOS\KEYBOARD.SYS /ID:166
LH C:\DOS\GRAPHICS GRAPHICS
C:\WINDOWS\MOUSE.COM
PROMPT $P$G
SET TEMP=D:\

MS-DOS Editor  <F1=Help> Press ALT to activate menus
```

Possible contents of AUTOEXEC.BAT in a DOS 5 or 6 version
(In the case of DOS 6 delete the second line of the file)

Remember that any changes made to the AUTOEXEC.BAT file only take effect after typing

    autoexec

at the system prompt, or after rebooting the system by pressing the three keys <Ctrl+Alt+Del> simultaneously, or using the RESET button on your computer.

Below we give a brief explanation of the commands used above.

The ECHO Command:

If in your AUTOEXEC.BAT file you do not have the command

@ECHO OFF

you will notice that every time you boot up the system, the commands within your AUTOEXEC.BAT file are echoed (displayed) onto the screen. To avoid such echoes, include the above command at the beginning of your AUTOEXEC.BAT file.

Following the echo off command, the path, keyboard, prompt and other commands are executed unseen, until echo is re-activated by executing the ECHO ON command. Using ECHO with a trailing message will display the message on the screen when a batch file is run.

The PATH Command:

It is more convenient to be able to use the MS-DOS external commands from anywhere within the directory tree without having to specify every time where the commands are kept (in our case, we have stored them in the DOS directory). The same could be said for the programs kept in the WINDOWS directory, the batch files kept in the BATCH directory, or the utility programs kept in the UTILS directory. This can be achieved by the use of the PATH command.

Whenever a command is issued, DOS searches the current directory and then all the directories listed on the PATH, for the correct file to execute.

PATH can only find program files, that is, executable command files with the extension .EXE or .COM, or files that DOS recognises as containing such commands, as is the case with .BAT files; for data files you must use the APPEND command as is explained on the next page.

Note the repeated reference to the C: drive within the PATH command, which allows the path to be correctly set even if the user logs onto a drive other than C:.

The APPEND Command:

It is conceivable that the software packages you will be using, require you to type a specific filename in order to activate them. However, some packages also include a second file (most likely a data file which might contain information about the screen display) which is loaded from the first when its name is typed.

In such a case, in addition to including the directory of the package in the PATH command within the AUTOEXEC file to point to the particular package, you must also include the name of the directory within the APPEND command, otherwise DOS will search for the second (data) file in the root directory, as its extension will most likely be .SCR or .OVL and will not search for it down the PATH. However, if the second file of a package is an executable file (a file with an .EXE or .COM extension), then you must use the **/X** switch after its name within the APPEND command.

In the display of the last AUTOEXEC file shown previously, the name of the BATCH directory was included in both the PATH and the APPEND command. This allows you to see the contents of a specific batch file, say those of DOS.BAT (to be discussed in the next chapter), by simply typing at the C:\> prompt:

TYPE dos.bat

If you do not include the BATCH directory in the APPEND command, DOS will not be able to find the file, unless you specify its directory after the TYPE command. Yet when you type at the C:\> prompt:

dos

DOS searches down the path, finds the file, recognises it as being a file which contains DOS commands (having the .BAT extension), and executes it. Position the APPEND command after the PATH command.

Other commands within the AUTOEXEC.BAT file carry out the following functions:

Command	Function
VERIFY	Turns ON/OFF verification that files are written correctly to disc.
GRAPHICS	Allows DOS to print on a graphics printer the information appearing on the screen when you press <PrintScreen>. The parameter GRAPHICS indicates that printer is either an IBM Personal Graphics Printer, an IBM Proprinter, or an IBM Quietwriter printer, while the parameter LASERJETII indicates that the printer is an HP LaserJet II. DOS 5 and 6 users, see the Help file for a complete list of supported printers (type Help Graphics).
MOUSE	Loads the mouse driver that comes with the mouse.
KEYB	Identifies the type of keyboard connected to the PC.
PROMPT	Changes the appearance of the DOS command prompt. The parameter $P forces the display of the current drive and path, while the parameter $G displays the greater-than sign (>).
SET	Allows an environment variable named TEMP or TMP to be associated with the string C:\TEMP. This is the subdirectory where Windows application programs create and later delete temporary files.

6. CONTROLLING YOUR SYSTEM

The DOSKEY Utility Program

MS-DOS 5 and 6 comes with an external utility called DOSKEY. This utility, when loaded into your system, allows you to recall the most recently entered DOS commands at the system prompt, for subsequent use, which can save you a lot of retyping. You will find that learning to use DOSKEY will be extremely useful to you in what follows in this chapter.

DOSKEY is an example of a special type of program, called TSR (terminate-and-stay-resident). Once a TSR is loaded into memory, it stays in the background without interfering with the other programs you are running. To load DOSKEY into RAM, type

```
DOSKEY
```

at the system prompt and press <Enter>. This causes a message to appear on your screen informing you that the program has been loaded into memory.

If you are going to use DOSKEY frequently, it will be better to include the line

```
C:\DOS\DOSKEY
```

in your AUTOEXEC.BAT file, which loads the program automatically every time you switch on your system.

If you have a computer with an 80386 or higher processor, you should load DOSKEY in the upper memory with the command

```
LH C:\DOS\DOSKEY
```

so as to avoid occupying about 3KB of conventional memory.

Once DOSKEY is in memory, every time you type a command at the system prompt, the command is stored in the DOSKEY buffer which is 512 bytes long.

To illustrate how this works, type the following commands, pressing <Enter> at the end of each line:

```
type config.sys
```

and after the contents of the CONFIG.SYS file have been displayed on screen, type

```
type autoexec.bat
```

and after the contents of the AUTOEXEC.BAT file have been displayed, type the commands

```
copy config.sys \batch
copy autoexec.bat \batch
```

The last two commands copy the two precious files into the \BATCH subdirectory, for safety's sake.

To recall the most recently executed DOS command, simply press the <↑> key. Each time this is pressed, the next most recently executed DOS command is displayed. In our case, pressing the <↑> key 4 times, takes us to the first command typed in the above example.

When the required command is displayed at the prompt, pressing the <←> or <→> keys allows you to edit the recalled command, while pressing <Enter> re-executes the chosen command.

Simple Batch Files

To complete the implementation of the hard disc, we need to create a few batch files which we will put in a subdirectory of the root directory, called BATCH. This will help to run the system efficiently. For example, we might require to know the exact name of a DOS command. This can be arranged by creating a batch file to display the directory whenever its name is typed. To illustrate this, first create the BATCH subdirectory, using the

```
C:\>MD \BATCH
```

command, then use **Edit** to create the DOS.BAT file in the BATCH subdirectory, as follows:

```
C:\>edit \BATCH\DOS.BAT
```

and type into the editor's screen the following:

```
@ECHO OFF
CD \DOS
DIR /P
CD \
```

then save the file. In line 2, the directory is changed to that of DOS and line 3 causes the contents of the DOS directory to be displayed using the paging (/P) option. Finally, line 4 returns the system back to the root directory.

However, before you can use the DOS.BAT batch file, you must include the subdirectory BATCH within the PATH command of your AUTOEXEC.BAT file. Having done this, save the changes and reboot the system, so that the latest changes to your AUTOEXEC.BAT file can take effect. Now, typing DOS displays the DOS directory, while typing any external MS-DOS command, invokes the appropriate command. A similar batch file can be built for displaying any other directory, the only difference being in line 2 of the file, which accesses the given directory.

Using Replaceable Parameters:

After some time has elapsed and you have written several batch files using the

```
C:\>edit \BATCH\MYFILE.BAT
```

command, where MYFILE.BAT is the batch file you are writing, you might find it easier to write a special batch file which itself calls **edit**, tells it into which subdirectory you want it to be created, and also adds the extension .BAT automatically for you. To create this special batch file, use **edit**, as follows:

```
C:\>edit \BATCH\EDITBAT.BAT
```

and type into the editor's screen the following:

```
@ECHO OFF
EDIT \BATCH\%1.BAT
CD \
```

then save the file as EDITBAT.BAT. Note the variable %1 in line 2 which can take the name of any batch file you might want to create. For example, typing

```
C:\>editbat MYFILE
```

at the prompt, starts executing the commands within the batch file EDITBAT.BAT, but substituting MYFILE for the %1 variable. Thus, line 2 causes entry into **Edit** and tells the editor that you want to create a file in the \BATCH directory, called MYFILE, with the extension .BAT added to it automatically.

As a second example, use the batch file EDITBAT.BAT, created above, to create a new batch file, which we will call ADIR.BAT, as follows:

```
C:\>editbat ADIR
```

and type the following instructions into the editor's screen:

Pre-DOS 6 users

```
@ECHO OFF
DIR \%1 |SORT |MORE
```

DOS 6 users

```
@ECHO OFF
DIR \%1 /P /O:GN
```

and save the file. The DOS 6 version of this batch file requests a directory listing to be paged (/P), with files displayed in sorted order /O, grouping directories first (G) and listing by name (N) in alphabetical order. This gives a better result, as directories are listed first, not included in the sort, as would be the case with the pre-DOS 6 version.

This batch file can be used to display the contents of any directory listed in alphabetical order of filename, a page at a time, by simply typing **adir** followed by the directory name. For example, typing **wp\docs** displays the **docs** subdirectory of the **wp** directory.

Special Batch-file Commands:

Apart from all the DOS commands, there are some specific commands which can only be used for batch file processing. These are:

Command	Action
CALL	Allows you to call one batch file from within another.
CHOICE	Prompts you to make a choice in a batch file, by pressing one of a specified set of keys, thus allowing you to build menus.
ECHO	Toggles on/off the screen display of commands executed from within a batch file, or displays the message that follows ECHO.

61

FOR	Repeats the specified MS-DOS command for each 'variable' in the specified 'items'. The general form of the command is:

FOR %%variable IN (items) DO *command*

where *command* can include any DOS command or a reference to the %%var. For example,

FOR %%X IN (F.OLD F.NEW) DO TYPE %%X

will display F.OLD followed by F.NEW

GOTO label	Transfers control to the line which contains the specified label. For example,

GOTO end

:end

sends program control to the :end label

IF	Allows conditional command execution. The general form of the command is:

IF [NOT] condition command

where 'condition' can be one of

EXIST filespec
string1==string2
ERRORLEVEL=n

Each of these can be made into a negative condition with the use of the NOT after the IF command.

PAUSE	Suspends execution of the batch file.

REM	Displays comments which follow the REM
SHIFT	Allows batch files to use more than 10 replaceable parameters in batch file processing. An example of this is as follows:

:begin
TYPE %1 | MORE
SHIFT
IF EXIST %1 GOTO begin
REM No more files

If we call this batch file SHOW.BAT, then we could look at several different files in succession by simply typing

SHOW file1 file2 file3

as the SHIFT command causes each to be taken in turn.

Combining Batch Files:

After you have created several batch files, one for each application you load onto your hard disc, plus several others to look at file lists in utility subdirectories you will realise that each such batch file takes up 2 or 4 KB of disc space, depending on the cluster size of your hard disc, even though individual batch files might only be a few bytes in size. To remedy this situation, you could combine all your batch files into one batch file, call it LOAD.BAT, thus saving considerable disc space.

It will be assumed here that you have 5 batch files which you would like to combine. These might be BATCH.BAT, DOS.BAT, and NORTON.BAT which produce a listing of the corresponding directories, LOTUS24.BAT which loads the 1-2-3 Release 2.4 spreadsheet, and QA.BAT which loads the Q&A integrated package of word processor and database.

Before we proceed with the writing of the combined batch file, we shall adapt the SHOW.BAT batch file discussed at the end of the previous section, so that we can obtain a listing on the printer of the contents of all the batch files we intend to combine into one, thus making our job easier. The new version of the SHOW.BAT batch file, which should be placed in the BATCH subdirectory, is given below.

```
@ECHO OFF
CD \BATCH
:begin
ECHO %1.bat
@ECHO OFF
TYPE %1.bat |MORE >PRN
SHIFT
IF EXIST %1.bat GOTO begin
ECHO No more files
```

Thus, to obtain a listing of the batch files of interest, simply type

```
SHOW batch dos norton lotus24 qa
```

and press <Enter>. Note that the SHOW batch file has been written in such a way as not to require the extension .BAT to be included after the entry of each of its substitution parameters.

Now, with the help of the listing of these batch files, you can proceed to write the contents of LOAD.BAT, as follows:

```
@ECHO OFF
IF %1==batch GOTO PL1
IF %1==dos GOTO PL2
IF %1==norton GOTO PL3
IF %1==lotus24 GOTO PL4
IF %1==qa GOTO PL5
GOTO END
:PL1
@echo off
```

```
cd\batch
cls
dir/p
GOTO END
:PL2
@echo off
cd\dos
dir/p
GOTO END
:PL3
@echo off
cd\norton
dir/p
GOTO END
:PL4
cd\123r24
lotus
GOTO END
:PL5
@echo off
cd\qa
qa
:END
cd\
```

In the above batch file, we assume that you will be typing the entries corresponding to the substitution parameters in lower case. For example, typing

LOAD qa

loads the Q&A package.

If you want to make the batch file respond to both uppercase and lower-case letters, then each line containing the IF statement must be repeated, as shown below:

```
IF %1==qa GOTO PL5
IF %1==QA GOTO PL5
```

and so on.

The CHOICE Command

With MS-DOS 6, you can streamline your batch files with the adoption of the **choice** command. The general form of this command is:

CHOICE [/C[:]keys] [/N] [/S] [/T[:]c,nn] [text]

where **/C[:]keys** specifies allowable keys in the prompt of the command. For example, if the following command is in a batch file

choice /c:bdn

what you will see on the screen is

[B, D, N]?

Adding text to the command, such as

choice /c:bdn Batch, DOS, or Norton

displays

Batch, DOS, or Norton [B,D,N]?

on the screen.

If you don't use the /C switch, **choice** uses YN (for Yes/No) as the default.

The other command switches have the following meaning:

/N	Causes **choice** not to display the prompt
/S	Causes **choice** to be case sensitive
/T[:]c,nn	Causes **choice** to pause for the specified nn (0-99) seconds, after which it defaults to the specified c character.

As an example, we have rewritten the first part of the LOAD.BAT file, discussed in the previous section, to incorporate the **choice** command, as follows:

```
@ECHO OFF
CLS
ECHO.
ECHO A    Display the BATCH Directory
ECHO B    Display the DOS Directory
ECHO C    Display the NORTON Directory
ECHO.
CHOICE /c:abc Select one -
IF ERRORLEVEL 3 GOTO PL3
IF ERRORLEVEL 2 GOTO PL2
IF ERRORLEVEL 1 GOTO PL1
GOTO END
:PL1
@echo off
cd\batch
cls
dir/p
GOTO END
:PL2
@echo off
cd\dos
dir/p
GOTO END
:PL3
@echo off
cd\norton
dir/p
GOTO END
:END
cd\
```

Notice that the ERRORLEVEL statements are listed in decreasing order because the statement is true if the parameter returned by **choice** is greater than or equal to the parameter specified in the IF command.

Finally, save this batch file under the filename CHOOSE.BAT.

Stopping Batch File Execution

To stop the execution of a batch file, press the two key combination

    Ctrl+C

or

    Ctrl+Break

more than once, if necessary. DOS displays a message asking you if you really want to terminate the batch file. Typing **Y** (for yes), terminates batch file execution.

* * *

DOS has many more commands which can be used to control a PC in special ways. However, this is an area which lies outside the scope of this book. What has been covered here should be more than enough to allow effective control of a microcomputer.

If you would like to be able to write customised batch files, create specialist programs with the use of the **debug** program and learn how to design your own professional looking menu screens, then may we suggest that you refer to either the book entitled *A Concise Advanced User's Guide to MS-DOS* (BP264), or the book entitled *Making MS-DOS Work For You* (BP319) also published by BERNARD BABANI (publishing) LTD.

* * *

7. GLOSSARY OF TERMS

Application
: Software (program) used to carry out certain activity, such as word processing.

ASCII
: 'American Standard Code for Information Interchange'. It is a binary code representation of a character set.

AUTOEXEC.BAT
: A file containing commands that are automatically executed on booting up a PC.

BACKUP
: To make a back-up copy of a file or a disc for safekeeping.

Base memory
: The first 1 MB of random access memory.

BASIC
: A high level programming language.

Batch file
: An ASCII formatted file that contains DOS commands which can be executed by the computer.

Baud
: The unit of measurement (bit/sec) used to describe data transmission speed.

BIOS
: The Basic Input/Output System. It allows the core of the operating system to communicate with the hardware.

Bit
: A binary digit; the smallest unit of information that can be stored, either as 1 or 0.

Boot
: To start up the computer and load the Disc Operating System (DOS).

Branching	Transferring execution of commands to another part of a batch file.
Buffer	RAM memory used to store data being read from disc.
Byte	A grouping of binary digits (0 or 1) which represent information.
Cache	An area of memory reserved for data, which speeds up access to a disc.
CGA	Colour Graphics Adaptor; 2 modes and 4 colours.
Cluster	A unit of one or more sectors. It is the minimum amount of space that can be allocated to a file on disc.
Code page	A table in DOS that defines which extended ASCII character set is used.
Cold boot	The process of starting your PC by switching it on.
Command	An instruction given to a computer to carry out a particular action.
COMMAND.COM	The Operating System's Command Processor which analyses what is typed at the keyboard and executes the appropriate commands.
Command line	The line on the PC's screen where you enter commands.
Command Prompt	The prompt (C>) which indicates that DOS is ready to receive a command.

CONFIG.SYS	A special file that allows the system to be configured closer to requirement by telling DOS where key programs are stored.
Conventional Memory	The first 640 KB of base memory, used by programs.
CPU	The Central Processing Unit; the main chip that executes all commands.
Current directory	The directory that is searched first for a requested file.
Cursor	The blinking line showing the place of the next input.
Default	The command, device or option automatically chosen by the system.
Device driver	A special file that must be loaded into memory for DOS to be able to address a specific procedure or hardware device - normally installed from the CONFIG.SYS file.
Device name	A logical name used by DOS to identify a device, such as LPT1 or COM1 for the parallel or serial printer.
Directory	An area on disc where information relating to a group of files is kept.
Directory tree	A pictorial representation of your disc's structure.
Disc	A device on which you can store programs and data.

Disc file	A collection of program code, or data, that is stored on disc under a given name.
DOS	The Disc Operating System. A collection of small specialised programs that allow interaction between user and computer.
DOS prompt	The prompt displayed on the screen, such as A> or C>, indicating that DOS is ready to accept commands.
DR-DOS	Digital Research's implementation of the Disc Operating System for PCs.
Drive name	The letter followed by a colon which identifies a floppy or hard disc drive.
Driver	A set of commands used to run a peripheral device (see device driver).
Edit	The MS-DOS screen editor which is used to create and modify ASCII formatted files, such as batch files, and the CONFIG.SYS file.
EGA	Enhanced Graphics Adaptor; 6 modes and 16 colours.
EISA	Extended Industry Standard Architecture, for construction of PCs with the Intel 32 bit microprocessor.
EMM	Expanded Memory Manager.
Enter key	The key that must be pressed after entering data.

72

EMS	The Expanded Memory Specification which enables programs to use Expanded memory, provided in DOS 5 and 6 by EMM386.EXE.
Expanded memory	This is memory outside the conventional RAM (first 640 K) that DOS uses. It can be used by software to store data and run applications.
Extended memory	This is memory above the 1-MByte memory address which DOS can use for certain operations.
External command	A command DOS executes by first loading it from an external disc file.
FAT	The File Allocation Table. An area on disc where information is kept on which part of the disc the file is to be found.
File	The name given to an area on disc containing a program or data.
File extension	The optional three-letter suffix following the period in a filename.
File list	A list of filenames contained in the active directory.
Filename	The name given to a file. It must not exceed 8 characters in length and can have an extension of up to 3 characters.

Filespec	File specification made up of drive, path, filename and a three letter extension.
Fixed disc	The hard disc of a PC.
Floppy disc	A removable disc on which information can be stored magnetically. There are two types of floppy discs; a 5¼" and a 3½".
Formatting	The process of preparing a disc so that it can store information. During formatting, sectors, tracks, a directory, and the FAT are created on the disc.
Function key	One of the series of 10 or 12 keys marked with the letter F and a numeral, used for specific operations.
GUI	A Graphical User Interface, which uses visual displays to eliminate the need for typing commands.
Hardcopy	Output on paper.
Hard disc	See fixed disc.
Hardware	The equipment that makes up a computer system, excluding the programs.
Help	A feature that gives you additional information.
Hidden files	Files that do not normally appear in a directory listing, such as the IO.SYS and MSDOS.SYS files.

HIMEM.SYS	The system file that allows the use of extended memory by DOS programs.
HMA	High Memory Area; the first 64KB of memory beyond the end of the base memory, which software can access.
Internal command	One of a set of many commands available to you at any time as they are loaded into memory every time you start your PC.
Interface	A device that allows you to connect a PC to peripherals.
ISA	Industry Standard Architecture; a standard for internal connections in PCs.
Key combination	When two or more keys are pressed simultaneously.
Kilobyte	(KB); 1024 bytes of information or storage space.
Macro	A suite of programming commands invoked by one keystroke.
MCA	Micro Channel Architecture; IBM's standard for construction of PCs.
Megabyte	(MB); 1024 kilobytes of information or storage space.
Megahertz	(MHz); Speed of processor in million of cycles/sec.
Memory	Storage elements organised into addressable locations that can hold data and instructions in a PC.

Microprocessor	A PC's calculating chip.
Monitor	The display device connected to a PC.
Mouse	A device used to manipulate a pointer around the display.
MS-DOS	Microsoft's implementation of the DOS.
Operating System	A group of programs that translate your commands to the computer.
OS/2	An alternative operating system to DOS.
Parallel interface	A device that allows transfer of blocks of data in bytes.
Parameter	Additional information appended to a DOS command.
PATH	The drive and directories that DOS should look in for files.
PC	Personal Computer.
PC-DOS	IBM's implementation of DOS for IBM PCs.
Peripheral	A device attached to a PC.
Port	An input/output address through which your PC interacts with external devices.
Program	A set of instructions which cause the computer to perform certain tasks.
Prompt	The System prompt displayed on screen, such as A> or C>, indicating that DOS is ready to accept commands.

Protected mode	The operating mode of 286 (and higher) processors, not normally used by DOS. It allows more than 1 MB of memory to be addressed.
Processor	The electronic device which performs calculations.
PS/2	The range of PCs first introduced by IBM in late 1980s.
RAM	Random Access Memory. The micro's volatile memory. Data held in it is lost when power is switched off.
Real mode	The normal operating mode of PCs, in which only the first 1 MB of memory can be addressed.
ROM	Read Only Memory - a PC's non-volatile memory. Data are written into this memory at manufacture and are not affected by power loss.
Root directory	The main disc directory under which a number of sub-directories can be created.
Sector	Disc space, normally 512 bytes long.
Serial interface	An interface that transfers data as individual bits; each operation has to be completed before the next starts.
SHELL	A front end to DOS or another Command Processor.
Software	The programs and instructions that control your PC's functionality.

SVGA	Super Video Graphics Array; it has all the VGA modes but with 256 colours.
System	Short for computer system, implying a specific collection of hardware and software.
System disc	A disc containing DOS' three main files and Utilities.
System prompt	The prompt displayed on the screen, such as A> or C> indicating that DOS is ready to accept commands.
Text file	A file saved in ASCII format. It contains text characters, but no formatting codes.
UMB	A block of upper memory made available by a 386 memory manager into which memory resident software can be loaded.
Upper memory	The 384KB of memory between the top of conventional memory and the end of the base memory.
VGA	Video Graphics Array; has all modes of EGA, but with 16 colours.
Warm boot	The process of starting your PC using the Ctrl+Alt+Del key combination.
Wildcard character	A character that can be included in a filename to indicate any character (?) or group of characters (*) that might match that position in other filenames.

INDEX

COMPANION DISCS TO BOOKS

COMPANION DISCS are available for most books written by the same author(s) and published by BERNARD BABANI (publishing) LTD, as listed at the front of this book (except for those marked with an asterisk). These books contain many pages of file/program listings. There is no reason why you should spend hours typing them into your computer, unless you wish to do so, or need the practice.

COMPANION DISCS come in 3½" format with all example listings.

ORDERING INSTRUCTIONS

To obtain your copy of a companion disc, fill in the order form below or a copy of it, enclose a cheque (payable to **P.R.M. Oliver**) or a postal order, and send it to the address below. Make sure you fill in your name and address and specify the book number and title in your order.

Book No.	Book Name	Unit Price	Total Price
BP		£3.50	
BP		£3.50	
BP		£3.50	
Name		Sub-total	£.............
Address:		P & P (@ 45p/disc)	£.............
		Total Due	£.............
Send to: P.R.M. Oliver, CSM, Pool, Redruth, Cornwall, TR15 3SE			

PLEASE NOTE

The author(s) are fully responsible for providing this Companion Disc service. The publishers of this book accept no responsibility for the supply, quality, or magnetic contents of the disc, or in respect of any damage, or injury that might be suffered or caused by its use.